The poetic musings of a lunatic

Victor Salgado

BookLeaf Publishing

India | USA | UK

Presentation by *BookLeaf Publishing*

Web: www.bookleafpub.com

E-mail: info@bookleafpub.com

ISBN: 9789363319714

First edition 2024

For my beacons

This work is dedicated to a group of people that are special in my life and I call them my beacons. Each one of them has inspired, encouraged and illuminated my path in this journey called life. To my wife Sonia G Salgado, babe, thanks for being Sonia, for being my light and my muse. To my daughters Jasmin Blackmon and Giselle Resendiz, you have given me unconditional love and the gift of being a father.

To my Father Victor M Salgado Pizarro Dad, you are simply the best, love you so much. To Anaira and Victor J guys, you know how we are and you know how we roll...Going along the railway, love you guys!

And last but definitely not least, two of my brightest beacons that keep shining bright from eternity, my mother Maria J Manso Rivera and my grandmother Georgina Rivera. Mom, Grandma — thanks for everything, always and forever.

ACKNOWLEDGEMENT

In this journey of life I have been blessed with superbly good travel companions. Beginning with the ones that brought me here Victor M Salgado Pizarro and Maria J Manso Rivera. Dad thanks for always having my back and leading me by example what being a man is all about. Mom, you may have left this plane of existence but your love, your words and your guidance are always with me, I love you. To my brothers Anaira and Victor J Salgado, who are not only my brothers but two brilliant and excellent lunatics that have never left me.

I'm indebted to my beautiful, darling wife Sonia G Salgado for always being by my side and believing in me and being my engine and the driving force that changed my life for the better, love you mamacita. To my first officer, bodyguard, big baby and friend my daughter Jasmin Blackmon thanks for everything you do for me, specially for the way you love me. To my pride and joy Giselle Resendiz for inspiring me to go for my goals and for making me your father, I will always be there for you. To my grandmother Georgina Rivera and my mother Maria J Manso Rivera for giving me the gift of rhyme. Thanks to everyone because without you this book would not have been possible.

PREFACE

The poems in this book are about the realities that compose life, family, inner dialogue and simply, being human. Many times sitting down and putting in words a feeling has been cleansing. There may be one or too spicy words here and there to really give flavor and resonance to a thing or two, just like in life itself.

Being a father

Being a father is blessing
No matter by blood or soul
Being a father is sacred
Is a mission from The Lord

We must not fail in the task
I know is a lot to ask
But if we think about the fact
We know we must stay on track

The fact is we are tasked with life
With making sure our kids thrive
And it is a task for life
To make them right and successful

And we all know is stressful
And sometimes is very hard
Nevertheless always blessing
Fathers, always stay on track

What is a mother?

The best advice
The realest love
A guiding star
When we're lost

Love without thorns
A warm embrace
Peace on the mind
To proceed well

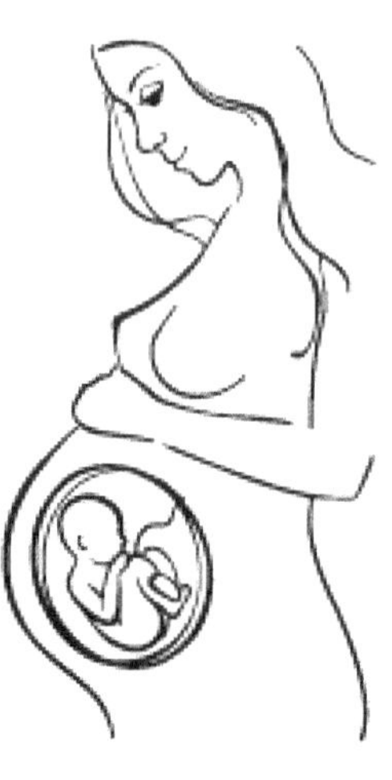

A mother's essence
Is love and peace
She'll always be there
They don't fade in mist

A mother's love
Transcends the void
Even from eternity
Mothers have a voice

Children

The children my wife gave me
They're an absolute treasure
It's like seeing our love
In human manifestation

Love is emotion and feeling
And it creates human beings
When I look at my kids
I see the power of it

Children are always blessings
Procure being ready to get them
Having kids is a serious task
To be done without a mask

Love your children with the soul
Because soon they will depart
To live their lives near or far
No matter, it breaks the heart

The family home

Where the food is good
Where we are in peace
Where we are always safe
Where the love is real

Where our life is shaped
The seed of our future
Where we grow and thrive
Where we get prepared

Is it a mythical place?
Or an enchanted forest?
Tell me, what is it?
Does such a place exist?

The family home
Is this and then some
For this very reason
Let's make it so in every season

To my wife

You're my friend, you're my love
You're a blessing from The Lord
You're my Moon and my Sun
The end and the pains of my soul

I remember the day of your arrival
For I was living without light
I just felt doom and gloom
But your love ended my plight

Life has highs and lows
Life has ebb and flow
This is true for me
You're my Moon, see?

Your gravitational pull
It's my driving force
You choose me every day
Love your light and soul

Of love and lunacy

Sometimes love is lunacy
Sometimes love is folly
Yet love changes lives
When it is real and holy

Sometimes it is lust
Disguised as love
Sometimes this will happen
And souls will feel lost

Lunacy is to love
Who we can't have

This is very horrible
And the pain will last

Love is many things
Is pleasure and light
But when love is lunacy
It becomes a blight

In dark times

In the dark times
We will be tested
In becoming whole
We must get invested

Dark times will come
This is simply a fact
And at this time
We need to shine

Look at the sky
During night time
Look at the Moon
There, shining bright

In those dark times
Be like the Moon
Go through your phases
And you'll be full soon

Friendship

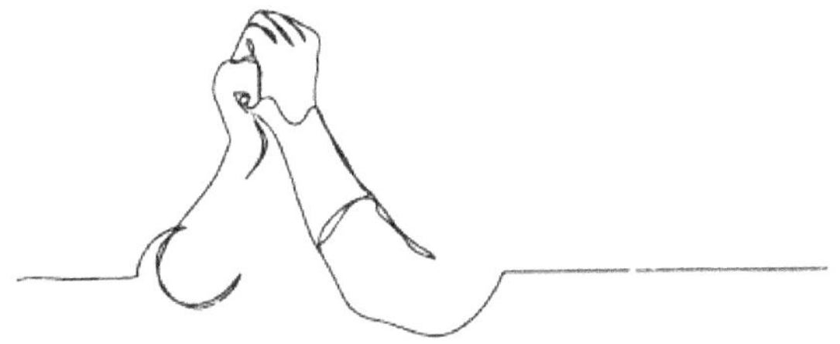

Friendship has phases
Just like the Moon
Sometimes be full
And sometimes not

Friendships can bloom
Like fragrant flowers
Can bring great beauty
Like the May showers

A real good friend
Is a great treasure
And this has worth
That can't be measured

Always be loyal
Always act right
Be always that friend
That's real and bright

The moon and the sea

One controls the other
One leads, the other follows
Is a great symbiosis
More than ebb and flow

With its silver glow
The Moon pulls the sea
The tide falls and rises
In a timeless dance

This a scientific fact
But let's cut the act
The Moon and the Sea
Is a cosmic love story

Time

What is time?
Where did it come from?
Where does it go to?
When will time end?

Time is a treasure
Use it for good
Manage it wisely
Teach this to youths

Where did time come from?
At this time isn't known
Use it to become wise
Do not be a silly clown

Time goes by fast
It goes to the past
It goes to be hard
And to have a blast

Time will end one day
In this plane of life
We'll go somewhere else
To restart the time

Music

Music is a vehicle
Is a time machine
Is a gorgeous language
It creates worlds within

Music feeds the soul
Also cleans the spirit
It focuses the mind
On the task at hand

Is a magic wand
It transforms the feelings
It creates emotions
Sets the world in motion

It speaks all languages
It spans the globe
It is and I'm very sure
A language of love

Wanderlust

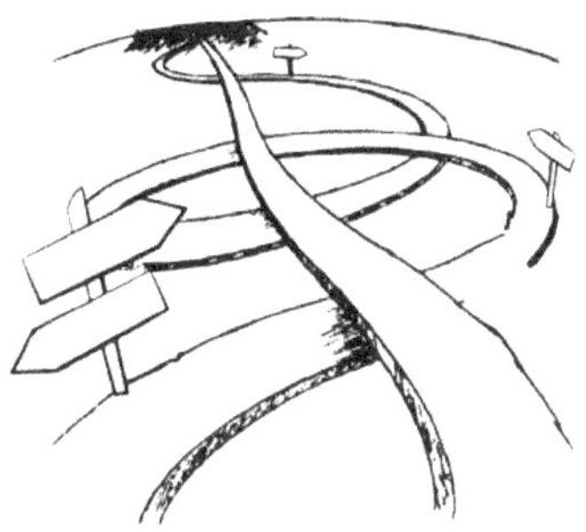

More than a word
A way of life
A true philosophy
A set of mind

It has its causes
And many roots
It holds one strongly
This is the truth

My dear friend
Go and satisfy it
Wander the earth
Go and see the planet

Create a plan
Go and execute it
Wonder and wander
Our awesome planet

Be the artist

Life is a blank canvas
Life is just like clay
Life is a blank page
Go and write your play

Become the artist
Turn into a playwright
Sculpt your life
Shape it bold and bright

Paint it with colors
Of vibrant hues
Unleash the artist
That lives in you

Sculpt your path
Write your story
Paint your legacy
With colors of glory

Winning

Winning, it is great
It will take great work
And it takes the craziness
Of defeating oneself

Defeating the excuses
Conquering our discipline
Looking at ourselves
With honesty and truth

Requires self-compassion
Also massive action
Unrelenting motion
Flawless execution

It requires belief
And trust in the process
Focusing on conducts
That destroy the losses

Loneliness

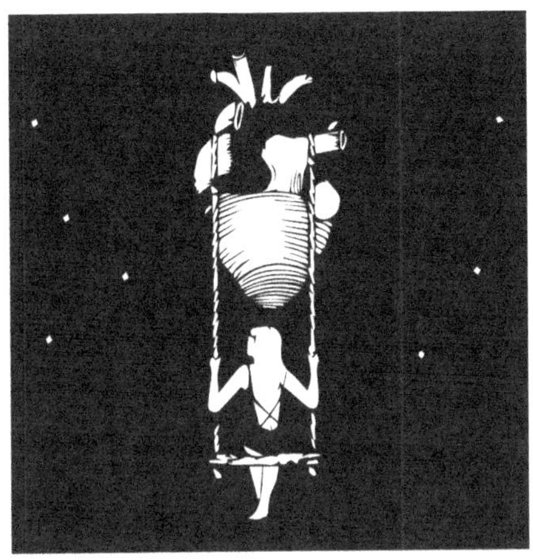

Loneliness is hard
Also can be fatal
It is a bad advisor
Because it clouds judgment

Loneliness may hurt
For years or moments
It will try to crush you
And become a torment

This bad situation
Has an easy fix—
Become your own friend
Cherish your own company

Why is this the solution?

Because it heals the soul
And a happy soul
Is sought out the most

Sometimes

Sometimes in family life
Strife makes a sudden appearance
And in that moment it is time
To end its interference

Sometimes some roles are reversed
Not by weakness but by need
But listen now and take heed
Always keep the respect real

For it simply doesn't matter
Who will cook, mother or father
Or which one will go to work
If we're together and happy

It's time for all to grow up
For the sake of this society
Because how will it be good
If we're messing up the family?

Together

Together, a beautiful word
When we want it to be true
If this way we want to be
But ugly when is not true

When a boy and girl so want
Together is, oh-so-nice!
But to be husband and wife
You must work to be together

You must not only work
It is precise to also need
That other soul in your life
Only if is true will you build

Build a strong and good connection
That will become the foundation
Of the family we all want
With love and communication

Moments

A good moment can heal
A bad moment can kill
This is a complicated fact
But both moments can do that

A good moment in bad company
A bad moment that brought agony
Both can heal and both can hurt
It depends on the situation

I'm being serious, these are facts
In a moment all can be lost
And a moment for years may last
A bad punch or a one-night stand

Take some moments to reflect
How in that moment you will act
In a moment all can be lost
And in a moment we can get on track

The past

The past is gone
Time to move on
Learn from the experience
An keep on going

The past is gone
Time to keep living
Leave it back there
And create the present

The past, it happened
Let go of it
Make new this happen
And you'll be happy

Learn from the past
Live in the present
Create a full future
Like the Moon in crescent

Distance

There are many distances
Both good and bad
Real or figurative
Distance is of life, a fact

Geographic distance
When we're in love
Hurts very greatly
Cripples the soul

Let's see the Moon
Far from the Sun
Yet reflects its lights
And with it, she glows

Let's be like the Moon
And let's reflect light
This way, being distant
Will never be a plight

Rivers

Rivers run to the sea
As I run to your arms
Your arms are my home
And your kiss is my breath

You're the queen of my soul
And everything that is nice
To me, you're a great prize
And to be yours is a privilege

You took me from the ledge
From the flood of the river
You gave me love and warmth
And you offered your heart

Sonia Gabriela, I love you
Like the Sun loves the Moon
Like the stars love the night
You're my river of light

The sea of tranquility

The sea of tranquility
Was what I wanted to sail
But that was an error
Doing it would've been a terror

Because the reality of sea
Is the reality of the sailor
And a tranquil trip at sea
Never made it a skilled sailor

It's necessary to have
Stormy weather at sea
For it teaches us the skills
To sail in the seas of life

So there you have it my lad
That the secrets of the sea
Can be used as well in life

Where

Once I was thinking
Where will I go?
When in my life
All is said and done?

What a great question!
That was for me
For long and hard
Eat my meat think

What happens to be
That the right answer
Was completely different
Than the one I was after

The time to live
The time to know
Is in the here
And truly now

I want

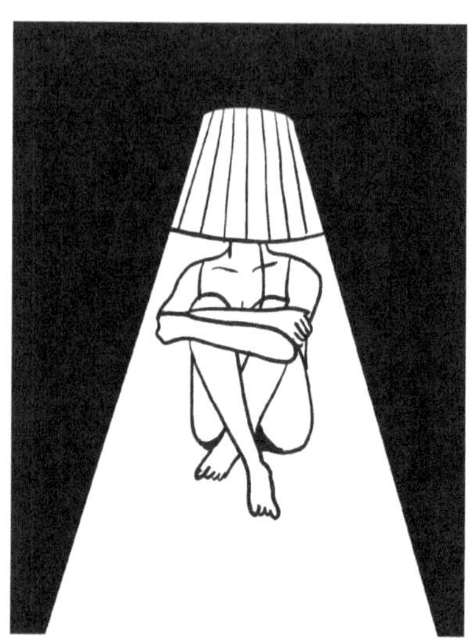

I want to be happy!
I will be happy when…
When you get A, B and C
Or perhaps X, Y and Z?

What is being happy?
Having material things?
Being happy is way more
And it comes from within

Doesn't come from a partner
Or from daughters or sons

It doesn't come from the outside
Happiness isn't a goal

Happiness is a decision
It is a state of mind
Happy people live better
And they are powerful and kind

To dwell

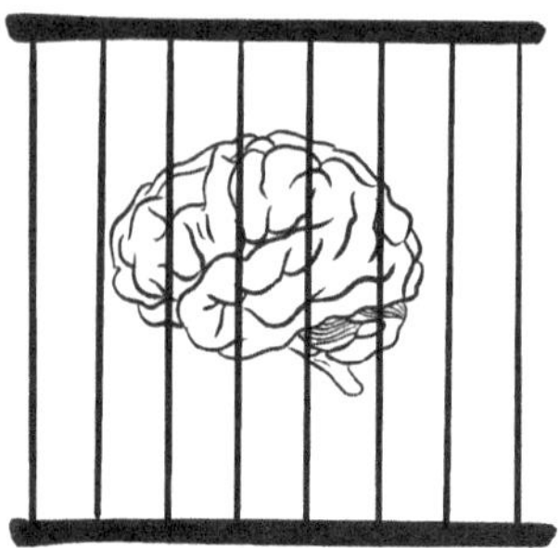

To do all means to live
And let me ask you this
In which part of your mind
Your dwelling today is?

Don't dwell on the problems
Don't dwell on the past
Clean out your mental house
A big anxiety and chaos

To do well in past victories
Is a sure path to defeat
Doesn't matter which feat
It is done and it has passed

Work on becoming better
On improving and growing
If you want to quit something
Quit dwelling and moping

Nothing

Nothing is sometimes a lot
Nothing is just evasive
When we avoid addressing
An issue that is pervasive

When we're asked what's wrong
And we simply reply, "Nothing"
We know that proper and well
We're indeed dealing with something

Nothing will bother you
If you take away its power

Do not give your attention
And it will give you no tension

Don't let nothing stop your roll
Keep on going nice and steady
Prepare your mind and your soul
And be always on the ready

Cause

What's the cause
What's the reason
Why the pressure
Why all the pain

Causes are many
As many as pains
And our decisions
Will alter them

Be a cause for love
Cause good impression
Do it with your true self
Don't use impersonation

Cause big inspiration
Be a cause of change
Because the truth is
There's no other way

Garden of night

In the garden of the night
You're the most beautiful flower
And at night I tend to you
My most fragrant and grand flower

In your petals I get lost
Under the shadow of night
Your fragrant is my delight
It smells of mystery and passion

You're my nocturnal flower
Yet you're also the queen of light
The colors that you possess
Are mesmerizing, the best

In the garden of my nights
I will always water you
For I want to see you bloom
'Cause you're my flower of love

Hours

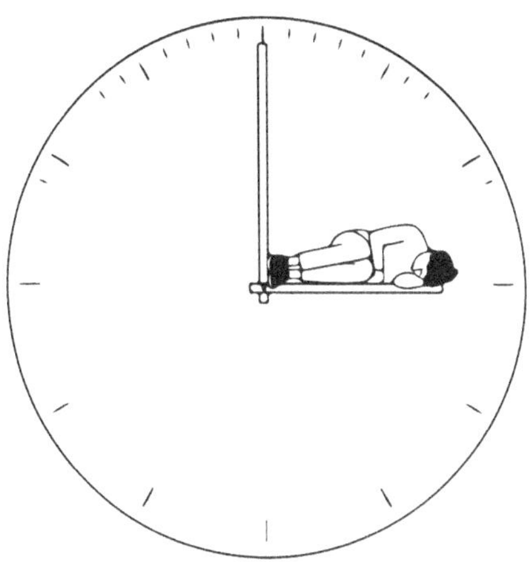

Hours are a measure of time
And can be fateful or idle
Sometimes that eleventh hour
Is the time to make or break

Sometimes we will say the phrase
"It's only a matter of hours"
With excitement or delight
Or fighting tears and fright

Hours can be so productive
But also they can be wasted
Time goes and never return
Value hours use them well

For one day, the final hour
Will strongly resound in our life
And at that moment in time
Is sweet to have had good hours

Innocence

Innocence is lost in life
For time and for many reasons
And also by our decisions
We find our innocence lost

Innocence, it is a virtue
And no longer appreciated
To many it's a laughing matter
It is a bother to some

When innocence is lost
There will always be a cost
Is not important to most
And in ways, it's now lost

Innocence by definition
Is a virtue as I've said
Be innocent as a dove
Yet cunning like a snake

Fear

Fear has power if we want
Fear paralyzes if we let it
It will stop us in our tracks
And keep us held back

The fear of the unknown
The fear of being alone
Or perhaps not being liked
Takes many blessings away

Do not fear the dark night
Do not fear being lonely

Because it is terribly worse
To be in toxic company

Keep the fear far away
Live with gallantry and strength
Be a force to be reckoned
And you will live very well

Quiet desperation

The quiet desperation
The night of the spirit
When pain creeps in
And we can't take it

Being desperate and quiet
Because nothing can be done
Because quite simply
We are broken and alone

In that quiet desperation
We need to focus on the quiet
And hear the voice of the soul
Because it will make us whole

Don't let desperation hold you
Become quiet and be calm
Take hold of all your being
And I assure you you'll win

The lunacy of sanity

This one is pure craziness
Or is it really? I ask
Because to live in sanity
A dose of lunacy is needed

Let's discuss why this is fact
From the real to the abstract
Sanity is always praised
While lunacy is frowned upon

Tell me that joining two lives
From a certain point upon
No matter where they're from
Do not require certain lunacy

The discovery of flight
And the speed of light
And even certain foods
Out of lunacy, they're born

So I have to say again
That sanity is overrated
Because to live with it
Lunacy has been necessitated

My woman

My woman is the greatest
She's indeed a soul of light
Life is beautiful for me
Because she's my guiding star

She's my peace, also my passion
Her hair, my favorite cover
When she smiles my soul is happy
Her voice is the song of my life

Her strength, it is formidable
And I know for she's my engine
She's this amazing great woman
But sometimes my little baby

My woman she is my world
She's my sun also my moon
And her love floods my life
Like the rains of the monsoon

Where to go

Where to go when it gets dark?
When life becomes really hard?
Darkness always will be there
Life is what we make of it

Where to go when love is gone?
When the heart becomes too broken?
When love is gone, just move on
The heart will mend if it's broken

Where to go when someone dies?
A mother, father or lover?
Death will always be a part of life
And who's gone is so forever

There's simply nowhere to go
That is not just going forward
The journey will get tough
And I will always keep moving onward

The other side

The other side of my eye
Holds images of the bygone
The other side of the pillow
Cools the fire of my nightmares

The other side of the fence
Where the grass looks greener
Sometimes is just a mirage
Because is fucking fake grass

The other side in a war
It is not always the enemy
But it is what we've been told
So we fight and will not fold

The other side of life
What is that thing called?
I don't even want to name it
'Cause it's been said it is cold

Sadness

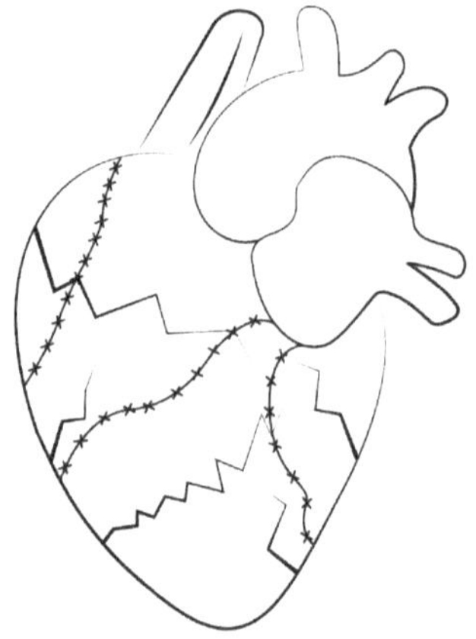

Sadness is a fact of life
Because it is what we believe
Maybe it'll always be there
But I just don't deal with it

Many things lose power
When we deny it to them
No matter if good or bad
This is a complete fact

That's why I say, choose wisely
To whatever power you give
To the things that help you grow
Or the ones that give you gloom

Is not a matter of doom
Is not a matter of fate
This is about making choices
So to you I say, choose well

Black and silver

Black is the color of night
Silver, the beautiful moonlight
Is a thing of great contrast
And that I like to focus on

The dark tint of the night
The silvery glow of light
Make me think of other things
That always make sense together

From a burger and a milkshake
To electricity and magnetism
And also, hey, why not?
Religion and mysticism

In this life, something holds true
There's no such thing as black and white
The colors that govern this
Are mixed and have many shadows

I am

I am a hopeless romantic
With a pragmatic mind
A citizen of the world
Proud of being a Boricua

I am a morning person
I enjoy being a night owl
I love chicken and fries
And of soup a hearty bowl

I enjoy being social
And love my solitude
I am not complicated
And for that, gratitude

I have many points of view
Yet I am a solid person
Always working to become
At all times my bestest version

A lunatic

A lunatic is not crazy
As an elephant isn't small
But lunatics are happy
For they live in their own world

A world according to them
With drums that sound like strings
A world that rains or shines
Will paint in the face a grin

A grin of great satisfaction
A happiness of the soul
Because the lunatic's world
Is one of wonder and splendor

You may not understand this
Allow me to explain it quick
The lunacy world is such
For the lunatic is the creator

Who enjoys

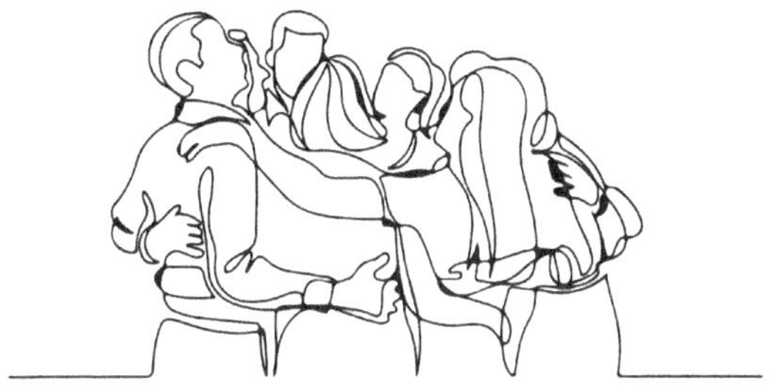

Who enjoys a sunset?
Who enjoys the rain?
Or the smell of earth
After such an event?

Who enjoys dawn?
Or sighting a fawn?
Seeing a baby yawn
While curling his hands?

Souls like that are few
Also very precious
If you know of one
You're indeed blessed

And if you're one
Go and spread the wealth
Enjoying these things
Is indeed a blessing

The insanity

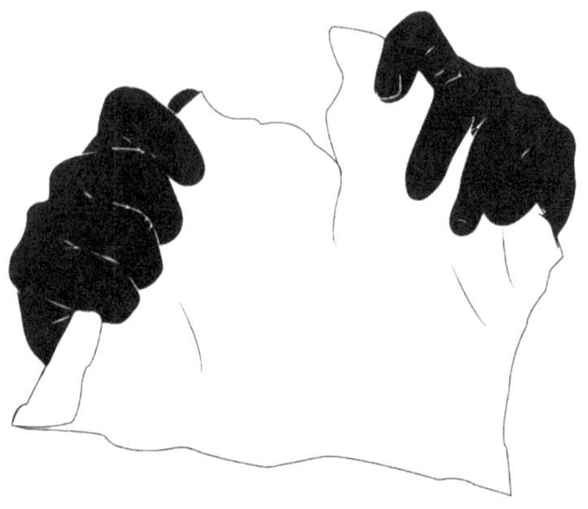

The insanity in this society
Is one that's kaleidoscopic
Because it colors everything
With colors that are toxic

These colors don't contain lead
But lead to many illnesses
Of the mind and of the soul
That people sometimes dismiss

I know you don't need examples
For samples are everywhere
From the elevated places
To the daily and the mundane

The insanity in this resides
Where we're aware of it
Yet we stay idle and do nothing
And we're going to pay for it

Of living

Of living and breathing
Of growing through pain
Of learning by struggle
Of winning by strength

By the strength to breathe
We struggle for the win
This toughens the skin
And fills us with strength

This life is an adventure
And living is a venture
That will end someday
For all this is the same

And for that same reason
I'll tell you on this day
Between now and then
Live life to the fullest

My adventures

My adventures are well, mine
And I would love to hear yours
With only one simple rule
There will be no competition

It's not that I lack ambition
But let's say like it is
When we're talking of adventures
Fantasy often intervenes

And when I mention adventures
These are not the racy kind
I'm talking of life experiences
Of the soul and also the mind

There will be no competition
For only a very simple reason
I want to hear all your adventures
But frankly, none of your exaggerations

To the point

To the point and that's it
What a boring situation!
Don't you wish to meander
And see what else is out there?

If we're talking about sex
You're just going to the point?
Or are you an avid explorer
Of the valleys of your lover?

If you're taking a road trip
You're just going to the point?
Or are you stopping on the road
To enter or smoke a joint?

The point is, beautiful souls
That everything has its moment
But always take one of those
To make the mundane uncommon

Of getting lost

Getting lost is many things
Can sometimes be terrifying
And sometimes getting lost
Is the way to find ourselves

I know it sounds paradoxical
And is a risky proposition
Yet my experiences in life
Made me take this position

Before every major break
On the way to every win
I have found myself lost
At the mercy of fate's whim

Yet at that precise moment
When I thought I was lost
I found the way and the manner
And always come out on top

In the moment

In the moment of truth
In that "AHA!" moment
What will be the emotion
Elation, guilt or torment?

The existence of the human
The times of the universe
Are not counted in years
It is counted in moments

Time is an expensive currency
Wasting it is total lunacy
But I have to say this
Its largest note is moments

Moments can make or break
Moments make and take lives
In the moment you get this
Your mind will really thrive

The pain

The pain of being alone
And the pain of being lonely
Are two different animals
And are equally destructive

But there's always an exception
And the opportunity is there
To turn these two pains around
And to finish their despair

If you find yourself alone
Learn to love your company
If you happen to be lonely
Then evaluate your companions

Alone and lonely is not equal
But they can equally breed
Self-reliance and resilience
Or bury us in a deep pit

Of the soul

My family that God gave me
Is indeed loving and great
And my family of the soul
Is a rich and loving blessing

To me, the thought is amazing
Because it's a perfect reality
Because I am truly blessed
With my two beautiful families

The family that God gave me
Taught me the meaning of love
And my family of the soul
Let me live the definition

Is mesmerizing indeed
That I am doubly blessed
With a double portion of love
Yes, I am family-obsessed

Is the darkest

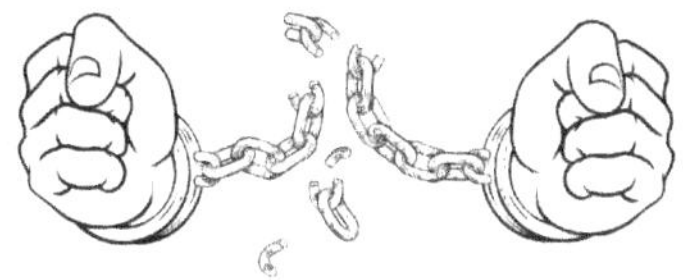

The darkest time of the past
The hardest moment of life
Simply became vaporized
When you took me by your side

I live in the blinding light
That your love shines upon me
And that's why, my dear love
That you're the one for me

Because you saw me in the dark
And noticed the spark of my soul
That little ember that remained
You changed to a roaring fire

And thus it is my desire
To always be by your side
Because you set my soul on fire
You make my life warm and bright

Me, myself and I

When I think of this phrase
A smile is born of my spirit
Not for egotistical reasons
But for a really big truth

I don't care if you're a youth
Or have reached old fart status
The reality of this phrase
Is a complicated apparatus

Me, myself and I are one of two
Either your biggest supporters
Or the three that will kill you
Complicated, isn't it true?

Now that you know of this
Work on these three individuals
Teach them the value of your life
And you will win over strife

Silence

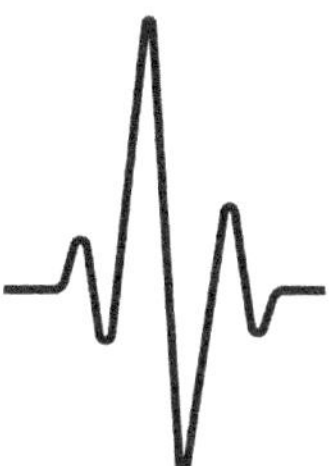

In the silence of the night
Is when the soul talks the loudest
When we have a silent spirit
Weakness becomes our language

We all carry soul baggage
Also we have spirit blemishes
So let's go to baggage claim
And then get some soap for dishes

Claim the baggage of your soul
And dispose of it properly
Take your spirit, wash it well
And let it shine in all its glory

Silence is not a foe
Is indeed a great tool
Because he who talks too much
Will easily become the fool

My yellow rose

You're my yellow rose
Absolutely my best friend
My new beginning in life
And from life, congratulations

You're my yellow rose
For you're my happiness
From The Lord, a gift
My biggest blessing indeed

You're my yellow rose
My queen of splendor
Your eyes are my stars
Your heart is my peace

My garden of wisdom
My queen and my lover
You're my yellow rose
My beautiful flower

In the blue

Something in the blue whispers
And I know to pay attention
Because that is your voice, Mom
Offering your wisdom and protection

Your voice comes to me in whispers
And those whispers are very loud
I listen to them inside my head
With your voice soft as a cloud

Something in the blue is beautiful
And that someone is you, Mom
With your voice like crystal bells
And your face bright as the sun

I know that you're in the blue
Is the only place big enough
To contain all your essence
And I feel you in my soul

Fusion

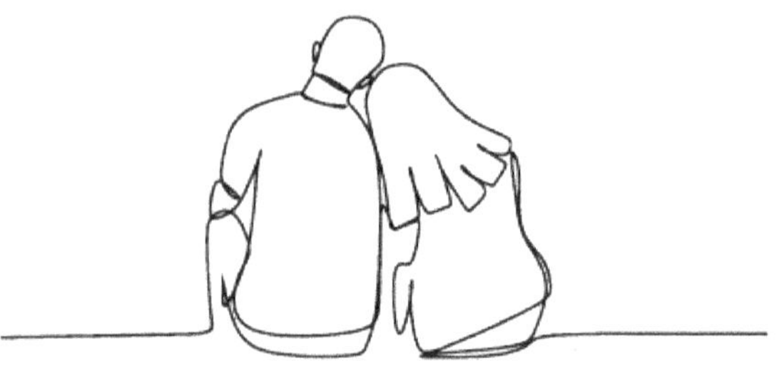

Your body is close to mine
And our minds begin to dance
I look at your eyes in trance
Is of the fusion the start

Fusion of bodies and souls
Also of minds and spirits
Taking flight to our sky
We soar together up high
\
Oh what a beautiful moment
When you fuse your soul with mine
Everything else disappears
As we launch into our sky

I want to always be with you
Because you're my twin soul
And I know it when we fuse
Denying it is of no use

Emptiness

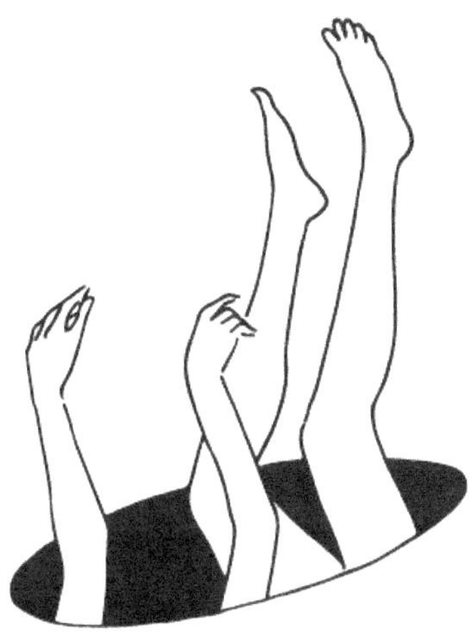

There are people in this world
With a hard and heavy problem
Nothing seems to fill their souls
And emptiness is that burden

There's always something missing
And there's always something more
The reality of this shit is a horror indeed
For them, being content is an awesome feat

Emptiness is their bread and butter
And they don't know nothing better
Do not try to make them happy
Became they will leave you empty

They fill everything with it
No matter how much you give
Their souls are bottomless pits
That will swallow and stay empty

Betrayal

Betrayal is bad and ugly
And it is a heinous act
Always comes from love
And that's a damn fact

But let's talk a lil bit
Because there are levels to it
Why does betrayal happen?
Sometimes we're forced to do that

Betrayal is sometimes an escape
And sometimes just a whim
But the truth of the matter is
We're all capable of doing it

The reasons are many and varied
And sometimes there's no excuse
The reality, my dear friends
Is betrayal is a fucking pest

I need you

I need you because I love you
And not the other way around
My life besides you, my love
Is peace and light throughout

You're a beautiful soul
And a very strong spirit
You're the stars of my night
My partner in this life

Sometimes I sleep and dream
Always dreaming about you
And in real life, my love
You're better than in dreams

Is a beautiful reality
The life I live with you
And babe that's simply why
I'll always be in love with you

Motives

Motives are just like human beings
Comes in all colors and shapes
Just like we all do sometimes
They can be right or all wrong

Be mindful of the motive
That makes you an action take
You may end up in a pickle
Because you thought it a piece of cake

Motives may determine outcomes
So again, always please take stock
If you're acting for shits and giggles
Or if your motives are strong

On one motive never act
One that seeks to hurt another
Just because you want it so
To be in that life a bother

Man vs Death

This is a fight that is rigged
There's only one possible winner
And it's been winning forever
And I don't think it will change

The fight of Man vs Death
Is rigged and we can't win
But there's a way within
And a mark we can leave

Live your life in a way
That when you pass away

You don't leave an empty seat
But a legacy that can't be beat

I'm not talking about assets
But of wisdom and of love
Because we can't defeat death
But we can love from the beyond

Kisses

A kiss can talk without words
A kiss can change a whole life
The betraying kiss of a friend
Or of a prince, the life-giving one

Like the last kiss from my momma
That left me a bit of her soul
Or the kisses of my father
That speak of strength and control

The kisses of my queen Sonia
That are of my life the music
Or the kisses of my kids
That are the fuel of my engine

A kiss can be many things
And I kiss with all my soul
No matter if it is of passion
Or of that family love

Committed commitment

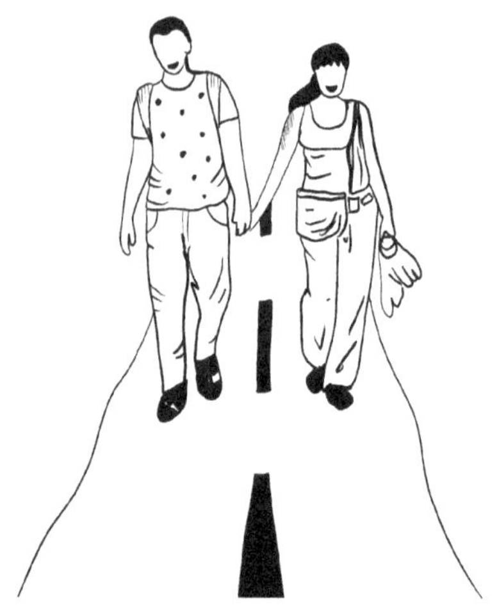

What is committed commitment?
Is it some kind of tongue twister?
Or just another invention
Of societal insanity? No, it is reality!

Real commitment, my friends
Can never be counterfeited
And sadly it often is
The symptoms are unmistakable

When a wife can't do the chores
When a husband can't provide
The shift in relationships
Becomes readily apparent

But when commitment is committed
Doesn't matter who will cook
Who will work to get the food
Or who will be the protector

Getting old

Getting old is a blessing
When we decide to live right
But it is very distressing
When all we've done is just fight

Fight because life isn't fair
Fight because we've lost
Fight because we've lived broke
Fighting even with ourselves

Getting old isn't maturing
And I know old bitter people
Who wasted their lives fighting
But not for the correct reasons

Fight to be someone in life
Fight to learn from your mistakes
Fight to have your independence
Then your old years will be golden

Location, location, location

If you don't feel appreciated
You need to check your location
Is easier for real estate
But it is the same equation

If you don't feel appreciated
Clearly you don't belong there
If you're only tolerated
It is time to leave as well

Location and appreciation
Share an indelible bond
When you're in the right location
You will know and doubt you won't

But first and foremost my friend
Learn to appreciate yourself
Because if you yourself don't do it
Don't expect it from someone else

Where is home?

About this simple question
There are complicated answers
But this question now for me
Has the simplest of the answers

Home is the arms of my wife
Is the laughter of my kids
Is the embrace of my Pops
And the memory of my mother

Is the voice of my lil brother
Is in the eyes of my sister
Is in the smell of the earth
After a summer rain

Is the memories I have
Of other lives years back
Is in the act of creation
Home is in a good vibration

Be the one

Be the one that makes a difference
Even in a single lonely life
Because we will never know
What change we can help to start

Be the one that is supportive
Of someone else's crazy dream
I'm not talking about money
But lend a listening ear

Be the one that helps someone
Because you were helped once too
Or exactly for the opposite reason
This will speak so highly of you

Be the one that is about it
And not other running mouth
Please do it for the right reason
Not for fame or chasing clout

The mirage

Be aware of the mirage
On the life of other people
For I assure you, my friend
It is just smoke and mirrors

And I'm not dissing or hating
I'm just speaking the truth
A lot of fantastic lives
Are a falsehood through and through

Procure to live in the real
Live in the present and now
Do not pretend to possess
The things you're struggling for

Live your life, always be cordial
In the struggle stay jovial
Deal with resilience and strength
The mirage will disappear

The lunacy of love

I have heard tales about love
I have read novels and legends
Have even heard once or twice
Love being called a demon

Love is a beautiful thing
And is not unlike the rose
As every rose has its thorn
Every love has its pain

And every love has its beauty
Also a lunatic phase
That can be an extended one
Or be rooted in recurrence

The lunacy of love is real
When also the love is so
If you have become infected
Don't you worry, enjoy it all

Full moon

As the full moon rises
My passion rises for you
The blood boils within me
I can only think of you

It is a horrendous pain
To be away from you my love
And when the moon is full
Is when it hurts the most

I want to see it with you
With my head in your breast
And hear the relentless song
Of your heart inside your chest

I long for your love my sweet
I long for being in your bed
And to receive the new day
Entangled into your hair

In

What is in, what is out?
What is life all about?
Chasing clout or money?
It's about not being phony

Is about going all in
About getting to the goal
It is about being true
To oneself and others

It is about having a word
And doing what we say
Is about being loyal
Overall, is about love

Love as in love yourself
And love your person
Love and adore family
That is enjoying reality